The Attributes
of G·O·D

© 1987 by
THE MOODY BIBLE INSTITUTE
OF CHICAGO

Each article in *The Attributes of God* appeared in the January 1985 issue of *Moody Monthly* magazine.

ISBN: 0-8024-0737-4

1 2 3 4 5 6 7 Printing/VP/Year 91 90 89 88 87

Printed in the United States of America

The Attributes *of* G·O·D

MOODY PRESS

CHICAGO

Introduction

When we speak of the attributes of God, we mean the distinguishing qualities or characteristics of the divine nature. These are not different parts of God's nature; rather, they are an analytical and closer look at it. They reveal the fullness, depth, and variety of His nature. God's attributes answer the questions: What is God like? How might we expect Him to act?

Can one speak with absolute confidence about this matter? Is not God's character really incomprehensible to a finite mind? His character is incomprehensible in the sense that God cannot be exhaustively known (Deuteronomy 29:29; Romans 11:33) and in the sense that He could not be known unless He had revealed Himself. We are dependent on the truth He has revealed about Himself to speak with confidence about His attributes or nature. His inspired Scripture has made knowable what otherwise would be incomprehensible.

Why has God revealed Himself? Why does He find delight in making it possible for man to enter into a relational knowledge of Himself? Think of the prospect of being perfect in every way—perfect in your love, your motives, and every aspect of your character. Would not the greatest privilege you could give someone be the privilege of knowing and enjoying you for who you are?

This is the heart of God, who actually is perfect in every way and desires for His creatures to experience a statisfying relationship with Him. Ultimately, our knowledge of God rests in authoritative Scripture, not in our experiences. But Scripture speaks authoritatively of individuals experiencing contentment (Psalm 73:25), security (Psalm 46:1-3), and great delight in God (Psalm 37:4).

Each of the eleven men and women who have written the following anecdotal accounts of God's attributes shares in the psalmists' emotional experiences. They write in the spirit of a psalmist, not as teachers or theologians, observing God at work in their lives. Their experiences reinforce Scripture, which assures us that the God who has revealed Himself is delighted to explain His revealed truth to us in a way that gives hope and direction to our lives.

BILL THRASHER
ASSISTANT PROFESSOR OF BIBLE
MOODY BIBLE INSTITUTE

*Richard S. Sisson is senior
pastor of Middleton Baptist
Church, Madison, Wisconsin.*

Transcendent
by Richard S. Sisson

As a young pastor in Nebraska I struggled to balance my formal, theological education with the imprecise world that suddenly surrounded me. Matters came to a head when I read in our local newspaper the tragic story of a missionary couple who were living nearby during a year of furlough. Their eight-year-old daughter had been kidnapped and murdered. Later, mangled pieces of her body were discovered in the trunk of a car.

I will never forget my sense of outrage. I was suddenly bitter at God for allowing this to happen. Such things may happen to Christ-rejecters but not to God's children. It simply could not be a part of God's plan. It took a long time before I realized that I faced a simple choice: either God was like me and therefore had made a mistake, or God was different from me, and I was in no position to judge His sovereign ways.

In my confusion Isaiah became my consolation. The prophet comforted his people by declaring the transcendence of God. "To whom then will you liken God?" he asked (40:18). He declared that God sits high above the earth He created. He rules over all. His is neither shocked nor surprised by the actions of men. World rulers are as "nothing" compared with His might and majesty. In contrast to His glorious perfection, people are as "grasshoppers" (v. 22). The unrighteous He simply blows away (v. 24). He is God, and beside Him there is no other (45:22). He owes us nothing. He controls everything. He reigns, tireless and inscrutable.

How kind God is to us when we face situations we can't control. In the midst of our panic His quiet voice whispers, "Do not anxiously look about you, for I am your God" (41:10). "Do not fear, I will help you" (v. 13). But this God does it His way, in His time.

Isaiah gets to the bottom line in chapter 46:

> Remember this, and be assured; recall it to mind, you transgressors. Remember the former things long past, for I am God, and there is no other; I am God, and there is no one like Me, declaring the end from the beginning and from ancient times things which have not been done, saying, "My purpose will be established, and I will accomplish

5

all My good pleasure"; calling a bird of prey from the east, the man of My purpose from a far country. Truly I have spoken; truly I will bring it to pass. I have planned it, surely I will do it. (vv. 18-11)

God asks us not to trust in what we see but in what we must accept by faith. We please Him when we rest alone *in the name of God* rather than our circumstances. Though His thoughts transcend our thoughts and His ways differ from ours, we please Him when we comfort those in difficulty by saying, "Your God reigns!" (52:7).

When we describe God as transcendent, we are calling attention to His radical "otherness." Though He has revealed Himself to us, it is a mistake to imagine He thinks like us. Though He loves us infinitely, we dare not believe we love like Him. Though we experience His grace, we would be foolish to take a moment of His grace for granted.

The apostle Paul described God as "the blessed and only Sovereign, the King of kings and Lord of lords; who alone possesses immortality and dwells in inapproachable light; whom no man has seen or can see" (1 Timothy 6:15-16). God is other because He is God.

Obviously our society is uncomfortable with this kind of God. That's why it has defined God. Now, it can truly be said that "there is no fear of God before their eyes." To be sure, people still talk about God. But the God of today is little more than a comforting word.

But does the evangelical church think of God any differently? More and more I wonder. I listen to Christians sit in judgment on God's Word. "I think the Bible is accurate in matters of faith but not in matters of science," they say. Others come into my office and complain that God is not treating them fairly. One person said, "I couldn't worship a God who does not permit women to be pastors."

What kind of God do you worship when your health fails? When your parents announce they are getting a divorce? When your son confesses he is a homosexual? Do you demand a full explanation? Do you say, "God, You have cheated me"?

What difference does it make that the God of the Bible is a transcendent God? I see four areas of implication.

DOCTRINE

Recently, I heard a radio preacher say something like this: "Some of you don't like doctrinal studies. But what is doctrine? I can define it in one word: doctrine is truth, and truth is doctrine. When you say you don't like doctrine, you are saying you don't like truth!"

Ten years ago, I might have had more sympathy for what he was saying. But not now. To be sure, God is a God of truth. His truth is perfect. But my understanding is finite, so I must confess I have not the capacity to receive God's truth with perfect understanding. Doctrine is the human product of trying to organize what we know about an infinite God. It is doing the best we can to come to terms with God's perfect revelation.

6

I recently met with an inquisitive Mormon student. He asked me how God could be one essence manifested through three persons. He wondered how God could die. He asked me why Christ did not know the hour of His return and how Christ could live in us if He was now seated at the right hand of the Father.

Such questions excite me to the core of my being. I feel a creaturely satisfaction in being able to say, "I'm not sure I can give you the whole answer. My mind is limited. God is infinite, and I am not. But let's turn to Scripture and wrestle together with what God has revealed about Himself."

Sadly, I find little charity in some Christian circles when interpreting difficult passages of Scripture. To receive their right hand of fellowship I must do more than agree about the essentials of doctrine. I must subscribe to all 168 affirmations in their doctrinal statement. If I can only affirm 167, I am shunned. No wonder Christians can't cooperate in many communities. Doctrine has been confused with truth. There will always be conflict when we sanctify interpretation rather than revelation.

CHRIST'S BODY

Have you accepted the fact that God may be at work in people who don't fit your expectations?

Open your eyes and your ears. See what God is doing. Our tendency is to brand those who are different as dangerous. How tragic when saints are exposed to only one guru, one "party line," one source of information, one reservoir of experience. Once I thought that God's program in the world centered almost exclusively on the local church I attended. But then I met people who didn't fit the mold. I had to make a choice. Would I adjust my definition of kosher, or would I ignore the truth I had seen?

Wouldn't it be just like a transcendent God to do an "end run" around traditional evangelical churches and in the last days accomplish His great work through a mighty outpouring of His Spirit in the mainline denominations? Don't limit yourself to comfortable labels. Open your eyes to God's handiwork. You may find yourself rejoicing in realities that once made you afraid.

TROUBLESOME CIRCUMSTANCES

Such is the greatness of God Almighty that He is able to use the fiercest enemies of the cross as unwitting tools of His triumph. Be they Chaldeans or cankerworms, God can use their wrath to praise Him.

What does this mean to the hurting believer? Though at present we see only pain, we accept by faith that our transcendent God is working out blessing through it all. "Therefore, let those also who suffer according to the will of God entrust their souls to a faithful Creator in doing what is right" (1 Peter 4:19).

WORSHIP

Evangelicals commonly emphasize preaching when the saints come together each Lord's Day. But where in Scripture is a sermon given such centrality? Constantly we read of saints praying and praising, sharing Scripture and the Lord's Supper. The early church gathered together to worship. I cannot help but believe that if we had a proper view of God, neither the stammering voice of an uninspiring pastor nor the off-key strains of an unprofessional choir could diminish the thrill of worship. We need to rediscover holy ground.

If God has become too common to you, make it your aim to rediscover His transcendence. If you have assumed the role of the judge of Scripture, the critic of the sermon, or the counselor of a confused deity, I pray that God will tap you on the shoulder as He did John. Remember when that exiled apostle got the word: "Come up here!"

Suddenly John saw the throne. The Holy One was sitting upon it. Every discouragement vanished. Every doubt about serving the Lord disappeared. In a split second of vision John was forever satisfied. The God he served was worthy of every sacrifice.

How satisfying life becomes when we know that the One to whom we have dedicated ourselves is so utterly worthy. Proclaiming His worthiness is the meaning of worship. God is worthy because He is other. He is Lord.

Mickey Day is a counselor at Montavilla Family Counseling Services, Portland, Oregon.

Eternal

by Mickey Day

About the closest any of us get to an encounter with eternity is being twenty minutes late to an important appointment and having to wait for a slow traffic light.

God, on the other hand, had to "adjust" to time. Eternity is to Him what water is to a fish.

Perhaps this great difference between our experiences of eternity is what led C. H. Spurgeon to say the study of God "is a subject so vast that all our thoughts are lost in its immensity; so deep that our pride is drowned in its infinity." Surely Isaiah was highlighting this truth when he wrote, "As the heavens are higher than the earth, so are My ways higher than your ways, and My thoughts than your thoughts" (55:9).

Be that as it may, because God's inspired Scripture is intended to make the man of God complete, "thoroughly equipped for every good work" (2 Timothy 3:16, NIV*), there must be some life-shaping truth here that He desires us to know. As mind-boggling as it may be, every man or woman of God whose goal is to be complete must ask: What is God's eternality? How does it shape my life?

It seems time is a bully who runs our lives, shoving away any "outsider" who might offer a solution to the mystery of time without end. Consequently, when we attempt to understand the concept of eternity, inevitably our minds fall into the hands of time. We can't fathom timelessness.

The creative mind of C. S. Lewis formulated a helpful analogy when he wrote, "If you picture Time as a straight line along which we have to travel, then you must picture God as the whole page on which the line is drawn."

Time a line, God a page! What a relief it is to know that the transformation of my life does not depend on the clarity of my understanding but upon my obedience to its clear directives.

God's eternality offered a refuge, a place of security and hope for His people, the children of Israel, as they faced the uncertainties of change through forty years of wandering in a barren wilderness. God's promise for a place of their own loomed large but unpredictable; they would encounter obstacles, and historically their attitude regarding opposition had not been good (Deuteronomy 1-3). The whites of the enemies' eyes darkened their memory of God's uniqueness. Such forgetfulness is inevitably the forerunner of failure, and what was true then is true today.

Moses addressed the Israelites' forgetfulness with a reminder that focused not on military strategies and the building of arms but on the eternality of their God. While such advice may sound foolhardy to ears more attuned to the beep of a computer terminal than to the voice of God, history supports the wisdom of His approach. The Canaanites are now relics of a distant past, but Israel and its God remain—and they always will.

Both scriptural and historical evidence suggest that the man who finds his refuge in the eternal God stands in an enviable position. In Christ we find our place of security, our hope, a refuge from all the unpredictable terrors of time. "There is none like the God of Jeshurun" (Deuteronomy 33:26), our God!

Though the Canaanites are gone, we who with Abraham search for that city "whose architect and builder is God" (Hebrews 11:10) find ourselves face to face with new foes and equally uncertain futures. Can old maps be trusted when our course takes us through the unpredictability of a job and income, children and parents, wives and husbands, brothers and sisters, family and friends, and even of life itself? Yes—when they are the production of an eternal God. To be eternal is to be above the uncertainties of time.

What may sound like one more pie-in-the-sky attempt to lend stability to an otherwise chaotic world has proved to provide me with exactly the security and hope God declared it would. Twenty-three years ago the course of my life joined with that of my wonderful wife, Sandy. Haltingly at times, though

New International Version.

9

surely, we have walked the path God set before us.

Our path, like yours, has led us through the terrain of normal family growth. The freedom of the young married couple soon gave way to the joys and frightening responsibilities of parenthood. And before we fully realized it, diapers and bottles had been replaced by first-grade readers and a host of outside friends.

The tempo of our trek then picked up to what seemed like blinding speed. It seemed almost impossible to see our "little girl" well on her way to becoming a woman and our "little boy" becoming a man.

The inevitability and yet unpredictability of our near future became clear recently as I sat at a wedding in our church and realized that our next big step would see us launching our own children into their future. Like all generations before us, our children will have to walk the same course we have just traveled. Strange new feelings welled up within me at that thought—new in quality, not in kind.

I had faced the insecurity and fear of an unpredictable future many times before. What was new was that never before had I faced it *for my children.* Would remembering the eternal nature of God work for them as it had for us?

Leaving our home to begin an independent though uncertain future was difficult for both of us. All we had for security then was imperfect experiences with our own imperfect rearing and an eternal God.

Our imperfections of experience magnified as we faced the possible death of a son born six weeks prematurely—but so did the perfections of an eternal God. Knowing that He who sat in eternity would welcome Sean home in grace, we gained security and hope as we weathered those weeks of hospitalization.

Finding the security of our home and its values threatened by an increasing number of authorities and friends during our children's school years was difficult. All we had for security was parental authority, lots of love, and an eternal God. Parental authority, however, was sometimes drowned out by a cry of "But, Dad, the teacher says. . . ." But never to be outshouted is the love that springs from an eternal God.

Introducing His love to our children, we saw them come under the shadow of His care when they received Christ as Savior. Their eternal God is above the changes of cultural values and mores.

The security of our family is now being threatened by yet another change. All we have for security is a growing relationship with each other and an eternal God. Hair that continues to turn gray (I'm discovering that gray hair is better than no hair) and skin that continues to wrinkle are constant reminders that death will one day postpone even the best of relationships, but the eternal God and all who trust Him will live on.

My life and probably yours stand with those of the children of Israel as testimonies to the security and hope that come to those who trust an eternal God. Wherever you may find yourself along your pilgrimage, whatever enemies you may face, rest assured: His eternal nature is the transforming span that will bridge the gap between learning and living the life of faith.

Calvin Miller is a pastor of
Westside Baptist Church,
Omaha, Nebraska.

A Person

by Calvin Miller

My car has just quit. No explanation, it just stopped. One minute the motor was going, the next it wasn't.

I felt an instant fury. I've never been good at expressing my anger to motors. They're so metallic and unresponsive. What bothered me most was the heater motor quit, too. The lights went dead—the machine was off, the temperature was twenty below, and the windchill index even worse.

Then I quit being mad at the motor, and I became angry with myself. I had left my overcoat at home, and my suit was one of my thinner ones. I got out of the car and raised the hood. Then I got back in and shuddered, dreading the thought of getting out again. I rifled through the glove compartment until I found a flashlight. I thought of the commercials that brag about the extra-long life of their batteries. With a gnawing fear, I pushed the switch on and smiled. The beam was pencil-weak, but as bright as a light can be on a dark night.

Each time I saw a pair of headlights in my rearview mirror, I got out of the rapidly cooling car and waved the light as a beacon in the blowing snow. Car after car ignored me as I grew colder and colder. Finally I flagged the beam at a pair of lights and smiled as they passed, for I saw the brighter red taillights that indicated the car was braking.

Only it wasn't a car. It was a pickup. It was filled, door to door, by two chunky and warm figures with sheepskin coats and gloves and ruddy warm smiles. "Lock it up and leave it," called the bristly driver. "I'll take you into Platte City, and we'll send back a wrecker to tow it in."

It was a commandment, and although it was not one of the Ten, I was too cold to disobey.

"Move over, Ma; give this young feller a little space between us."

I felt odd moving in under the long gear shift, but the toothy grin of his wife convinced me I was welcome—only not in far enough, for he scooted me next to his mate, and I laughed even as he laughed.

"Thanks so much," I said. "I wanted to make it to Omaha."

"Omaha! That's a hundred and sixty-five miles," he said. "You better settle for Platte City. You bust your car down north of Mound City, and I guarantee you there won't be much help along this time of night."

11

"Omaha!" his wife spoke aloud in my frozen right ear. "Sonny, honey, you better get warm, and then we'll take you where you spend the night. Didn't your mama ever tell you how to dress on cold nights?"

"Uh huh." I felt ashamed to answer yes.

"Well, Sonny, honey, you be smart to pay attention to your mama."

"Yes, Ma'am." I grew quiet. My two huge companions wedged me into warmth, and I felt like maybe I was going to survive. The missus felt my hand.

"Sonny, honey, you're going to have frostbite." It was a rebuke, but not the kind that was mean, only sympathetic with my hurt.

In a very real way the couple had saved me—probably from myself—from exposure to a blizzard that showed no signs of letting up.

How shall I liken this couple to God as a person? Here was a pickup driver whose formal education and personal appearance were lacking. Yet in so many ways he reminded me of majesty—yes, ever-saving majesty—the great and personal God who behaved toward me as the saving person. How like God. He came to me, seeing my need, and stopped for me when no one else would.

He ordered me to warmth and life and carried me next to his own warming and protecting presence. He offered me rebuke and correction out of the concern he felt for me. Between these two large people I felt surrounded by personhood. "God is a Spirit: and they that worship him must worship him in spirit and in truth" (John 4:24, KJV*). God is an omnipotent being whose personhood not only fills us but also surrounds us.

He related to me in a personal way and communicated to me as a person. God desires to communicate with us. Persons are communicative beings. They speak, listen, and build relationships. So it was that night with my benefactors.

There is another attribute of God. He has a name by which He discloses Himself to us. My friend's name was Jim; I can't remember at what point in our conversation I learned that, but it was Jim nonetheless. His deliverance that cold night was extra special because we were on a first name basis.

There was a lot of theology hidden in that simple act of kindness. I guess there always is. Oh, yes, there's one other personal attribute of God. He keeps His promises.

Naturally Jim kept his promise to get my car working again. It seemed my whole life worked better after that night.

*King James Version.

*Rebecca Manley Pippert is a
conference speaker and
author in Tel Aviv, Israel.*

Faithful

by Rebecca Manley Pippert

"This has been a tough year," commented a friend I admire. "But I've decided what God is up to in my life. In a thousand different ways, He is building my character. So, looking at life through that lens, I'd have to say it's been a painfully good year. My daily prayer has become, 'O Lord, make me a faithful man.' It saddens me to see how little value Christians place on building character."

Character and faithfulness have never been high commodities in a faithless generation. For aren't we guilty of being dazzled by glitter more than substance? Or of secretly desiring the "up-front" gifts or of idolizing those who have them? God gave us the desire for significance for His glory. But when significance has come to mean simply being noticed, we're in trouble.

In a commencement speech, Garry Trudeau, author of the cartoon strip *Doonesbury,* said, "You will find your worth is measured not by what you are, but by how you are perceived. There is something disturbing in our society when men wish not to be esteemed, but to be envied. . . . when that happens, God help us."

The significance God desires for us is godly character, and one attribute of His character is faithfulness.

The psalmist tells us God's faithfulness is as firm as the heavens (Psalm 89:2). We can count on Him. "I will not take my love from him, nor will I ever betray my faithfulness. I will not violate my covenant" (Psalm 89:33-34, NIV). God has made an oath to us, and He will not break it. He will be faithful to us; to do otherwise would be to violate His very nature.

Again and again the Bible reminds us that God is worthy of our trust. He will not withhold His loyalties and affection from us in favor of other interests. He stands by His promise.

Yet while God's faithfulness can bring us tremendous comfort, it can also bring great discomfort, for the world should see His faithfulness demonstrated in how we live our lives. We are to reflect His character.

Why is it so difficult to be faithful? Because it's hard work; there is nothing glamorous about learning godliness. It involves the destruction of self-seeking as we learn to seek God, and who among us is eager to die?

13

I have found that doing a speaking tour is a piece of cake next to learning how to be a loving, unselfish, faithful, godly wife. Preaching dogma is easy; living it is another matter. Making a connection between truth I believe and truth I really live—that's what builds faith and character.

But the process of acting on what I know to be true involves not only hard work but also pain. And if you're like me, you'll do anything to avoid the pain of facing yourself. We overspiritualize and seek to live on a higher plane, claiming victory when in fact we are denying our problems.

Or we try to remove the pain. We certainly have the freedom to ask that our problems be removed. Jesus did it in Gethsemane. In His case, God's answer was no. Sometimes God's answer is yes, and we can thank Him for that. But the test of God's faithfulness does not depend on whether He removes the pain or problem.

The third option in facing this inevitable costly pain is to resolve to become the person He wants, no matter what. God's grace will be sufficient for the evil of the day. No matter how battle fatigued, how sick and weak we feel, He will not allow us to be tempted beyond what we can bear.

Sometimes God's faithfulness is seen in how He removes the pain or problem and gives us what we've longed for. Other times His faithfulness is seen in how He does not give us what we request, how He sustains us and molds us through the suffering. The Christians who have helped me most are those who have said, "This is how God has met me in my brokenness. I'm still suffering, but His presence and comfort are real and have sustained me. At the deepest level of my self, He has enabled me to be faithful, even though He hasn't eliminated the problem." We need to hear both sides of His faithfulness.

Never have both sides been more real to me than on a recent speaking tour. For five years Wes and I hoped and prayed for a child. Finally, last year, we became parents. From beginning to end, Elizabeth's birth was a story of God's faithfulness.

I didn't discover I was pregnant until I was three-and-a-half months along. What I had assumed was normal each month was in fact hemorrhaging from a detached placenta. We were told a miscarriage was likely.

I was immediately hospitalized and confined to bed. Five days later I nearly lost the baby. The hemorrhaging was so intense the doctors feared I might go into shock, and they thought they might have to do a dilatation and curettage before the day was over. But then, as suddenly as the intense bleeding had started, it stopped. One month later, I went home.

We began receiving letters from Christians from all over the world who said they were praying that the placenta would stay attached and that I'd give birth to a healthy child.

During those months I experienced many stages of emotional highs and lows, times of gripping fear and despair, times of great peace and rest in God. Most of all, it was a time of learning to trust. I poured out my fears and deepest desires to God. The Scriptures that helped me most were those that dealt with His faithfulness.

Scripture gave me the assurance not that we always get exactly what we ask for but that we are in the Lord's hands. He is worthy of our complete trust no matter what the results.

When the time came to deliver, I had my first contraction at 3:30 A.M. and things began to move quickly. I later discovered I went through every stage of labor in sixty minutes. My only vivid memories are when Wes rushed me to the hospital and stopped on the way to buy a newspaper (the joy of being married to a journalist).

There hadn't been time to call our doctor or Irene (a Jewish Christian), my midwife who had seen me through the whole pregnancy; I had wanted her at my side for the delivery.

As we walked into the hospital at 5:10, I saw Irene standing before us. "What are you doing here?" I shrieked.

"Becky, this is the only night shift duty I've had in two weeks. God doesn't play games with His children. He knew you wanted me here."

She rushed me into the delivery room, and twenty-two minutes later I was holding Elizabeth in my arms. If Wes and I have ever known outrageous, ecstatic joy, it was at 5:37, January 24, 1985.

There was only one complication in the entire labor experience. My placenta wouldn't come out. When it finally did, Irene showed Wes where it had detached and turned brown.

"But why is the rest so torn up?" he asked.

"Because the placenta simply would not detach itself from Becky."

"I'm not surprised," Wes said. "Do you have any idea how many prayers went up for this organ?"

As I lay there holding our daughter, I realized that they were examining something that had lived inside of me and nourished our baby. Now visible, it was demonstrable proof that God is faithful. He had answered the prayers of so many. For the first time that morning, I wept.

On a recent speaking tour I told this story. Later that same morning another speaker told hers. She had six miscarriages, one at six months, and three failed adoptions. Still childless, she was not past child-bearing years.

Speaking to me privately, she said, "Becky, don't feel sorry for me. God *has* been faithful to me. In the toughest times His comforting presence saw me through. He has given me spiritual children and a life far better than I could have imagined. He's always proved Himself worthy of my trust.

"I'm glad we were able to share our stories at the same time. People need to hear both stories and then praise God for His goodness and faithfulness no matter what."

Reality and spiritual strength carried her words; there was nothing saccharin or falsely pious. It was the real thing.

God is God. His faithfulness does not depend on our goodness or gimmicks. His grace is available to strengthen us so we may live as a faithful people in a faithless generation no matter what.

"I will sing of the lovingkindness of the Lord forever; to all generations I will make known Thy faithfulness with my mouth"—and my life (Psalm 89:1).

Ruth Senter is editor of
Partnership *magazine.*

Just

by Ruth Senter

I watched the sun filter through the ancient oaks of Wisconsin's Kettle Moraine area. The early morning light slipped silently from branch to branch. The couple in the neighboring tent watched the same sunrise through bleary eyes and pulsing vibes from their ghetto blaster.

"They couldn't be more than sixteen," I said to my husband, Mark, as we climbed the hill for water. We both doubted the legitimacy of their night together. But the sun, that celestial goddess of all Wisconsin campers, shined just as brightly on their side of the oaks as it did on ours. And hours later, when the clouds gathered and the heavens descended, we were pelted just as hard with the driving rain. Never mind that I'd just spent thirty minutes in the book of Isaiah while the neighbors guzzled more beer and rocked to the Beatles. The rain falls on the just and the unjust (Matthew 5:45).

"God is fair," I said to myself as I walked away, "whether or not I understand His ways." Nature, that neutral agent of distribution, showed no partiality.

Today I rode my bike down the street to the gold house on the corner of Thunderbird and Blackhawk. Death was in that place. I felt it as soon as I stepped inside. Beth's wheelchair was folded by the door; her cane hung on the closet doorknob. "She's too weak to even use them anymore," her mother said. "We haven't walked in a week." Tears gathered in her blue eyes, and I tried to swallow the tightness in my throat. But I couldn't make it go away.

I wished I could make it all go away—this ugly nightmare of an inoperable brain tumor that sucked life from a fourteen year old. I couldn't help but notice the family picture that hung above the living room couch. In it is the Beth of nine months ago—a track star in full bloom. Now the petals are shriveled. The flower faded. "Beth talks about heaven," her mother said. The neighbor asked, "How could this happen to folks like you who go to church every Sunday?"

"God is fair," I said to myself as I walked away, "whether or not I understand His ways." And pain, that neutral agent of distribution, fell on the just and the unjust.

I see the sun rise. I feel the pain. And I witness the impartiality of it all. No respecter of persons. But then, why should I expect anything different?

16

Nature reflects the One who created it. God is a just God, One who shows no partiality. Outside of grace, God's penalty falls on all. "The wages of sin is death" (Romans 6:23). Sin is sin. The consequences have been posted; He gives fair warning. No excuses accepted. No variations on the rules. Man is accountable. Rebellion, be it active or passive, calls for justice.

I understand God's justice because I remember rebellion—ten-year-old rebellion. My father was the dispenser of justice. "No swimming in the creek today," he said. I had plenty of excuses: "Jimmy went in." "I was so hot." "It isn't fair when everybody else's dad lets them go."

Excuses didn't matter because the standard had been violated. The penalty was swift and sure. Justice was done. But then the father who had just administered justice reached for his big white handkerchief and wiped the tears from his eyes. That day, justice and love were forever linked in my mind.

My father's actions pointed me toward a heavenly Father who sits in the hall of justice, calls His creation to accountability, but weeps over waywardness even as He pronounces sentence. "Oh, Jerusalem, Jerusalem . . . how often I have longed to gather your children together, as a hen gathers her chicks under her wings, but you were not willing!" (Luke 13:34, NIV). Justice and love exist in the same person.

The sun rises on both sides of the camp. Rain falls on the tents of the godly and the ungodly. Pain is no respecter of persons. Neither is God. Sin contaminates all, and grace is available to all, no matter who stands before the bar. I can be at peace about God's system of justice, for I have confidence in the Judge. There will be no payoffs. He judges clean.

As a sinner who knew where to find grace, I know God today not as my judge but as a loving Father who continually calls me to accountability. One day He was my judge. But I can almost see a white handkerchief dabbing tears as He wept over my rebellion, issued the sentence, and then took my penalty upon Himself. I am acquitted. Justice has been done. My debt has been paid. I can rest my case. But somewhere in Wisconsin, the sun still shines on the tents of the ungodly and down the street a fourteen year old withers away.

"God is fair," I said to myself, "whether or not I understand His ways. For He is a God of justice."

Jill Briscoe ministers with her pastor-husband, Stuart, at Elmbrook Church, Brookfield, Wisconsin.

Love

by Jill Briscoe

I was eighteen and not a believer when someone told me that God is love and that His love had been demonstrated dramatically in Christ, shaped by His cross. To understand how such sacrificial love worked, I would need to know this giving God for myself and ask Him to lend me, by His Spirit, His divine ability to love others irrespective of their responses or reactions. I received Christ and asked Him to do just that.

At first it was difficult to admit I needed help loving. After all, I was eighteen and in and out of "love" almost every week. But I came to understand from the Bible that *eros,* the feeling part of love, ebbs and flows like the tide, but God's *agape* love is like the sands of the seashore—it endures forever. What's more, it remains whether the tide is in or out.

Had not God decided to love us to the end? I reckoned He had not felt like hanging on the cross, but He obeyed anyway, knowing that real love remains steadfastly determined to act in love whatever the cost.

Before I knew the Lord, I had realized with sadness that even the wonderful *phileo* family love I had been privileged to know too often had been tinged with selfishness on my part, while the best of the friendships I enjoyed were at the mercy of the waves of my emotions. In other words, when the feelings ran out, so did I—on the boyfriend or girl friend. It mattered not; after all, I reasoned, nobody expects anyone to continue "trying" to get along with someone if he doesn't feel like it.

Now that I had become a committed Christian, it came as a considerable shock to discover that Jesus *did* expect me to get along with others when I didn't feel like it. In effect, God was commanding me to act lovingly with or without the feelings. In practical aspects, loving "God style" began to complicate my life.

Before knowing God, I had no problems liking those who liked me or loving those who loved me. "So what," Jesus indicated, apparently unimpressed. "Even sinners do that" (Luke 6:32-33). It became obvious that the Lord expected more from His friends.

As I began to grow in the Lord and reread the gospels, I observed that

18

Jesus loved His enemies—He prayed for His tormentors; He called Judas "friend." This same Savior was promising me the power to obey His command to love as He loved (John 14:23). He had the power to free me from my selfish love and enable me to love those I didn't feel like loving. After all, He had lived on earth; He knew how hard people were to love.

The first test came when I left Cambridge as a young adult and mingled with street-wise students in Liverpool in the course of my teaching profession. That led to late nights, a little danger, and exposure to a strange new world of flashing lights and thumping music, not to mention the strangely garbed creatures huddling in the corners of coffee bars and drug dives. This world provided me with plenty of opportunities to love kids who need loving. Doing love instead of just feeling love meant costly involvement.

A commitment to love *agape* style—whatever, wherever, however—led my husband and me to share our small home with troubled teenagers who munched our food, slept in our beds, invaded our privacy, and sometimes broke or spoiled our possessions. The carpet wore out, and the couch grew grubby as kids we didn't particularly *feel* for, and certainly would never have picked for our friends, took up residence in our residence and later—much later—in our hearts.

Other tests came years after when our own children burst into adolescence like comets looking for a place to crash. This was a time when *eros* tended to rule their behavior and their mother's response. In those days, loving God's way meant being kind instead of cutting, picking up the living room after a teenage war, running the errand or washing the blouse, or even helping the kids with some of the very chores we'd given them in the first place. I discovered then that loving when I didn't feel like loving pleased the Lord and pleased them.

Did we spoil them? Maybe. But in the long run those sorts of practical loving actions enlarged me as a person and many times bridged the gap in our family relationships.

Of course, it wasn't always a one-way street. Many times I have been the blessed recipient of such real love from my own children.

I can remember one incident when my daughter who was at college insisted on spanning the chasm of conflict between us by calling me long-distance. I was sitting at home at the time, shrouded in silence, enjoying a pout. In that instance, love took the initiative, lifted up the phone, and said, "Hi, Mom. Wish you could see my little white flag—I'm surrendering. It's not worth the bloodshed, the wounds, the tears . . . because I love you."

She didn't need to do that. But love does things it doesn't need to do.

As I studied God's love in Christ through Scripture, I understood that love is essentially concrete and practical. It is character in action. Jesus manifested incredible love in terms of "people patience," kindness, and self-control. He was always looking for ways to be constructive. I began to look for them.

Christ lived a life of love, content to refuse the trappings of trivia in order to better share Himself with others. So I, too, learned to work toward a more simple life-style. I saw that love and humility are sisters who behave courteous-

19

ly at all seasons and that a truly loving mind refuses access to plans of revenge. Love doesn't get even because it is too busy making peace.

As a pastor's wife, I've asked God to help me be a mediator, not a gladiator. Jesus always looked past a person's sins to his potential, believing the best about him even when everyone else believed the worst. I've asked love to change me from a negative to a positive person, just as He is. Jesus never became touchy, or supersensitive; love doesn't take everything personally.

Over the years it has become abundantly obvious to me that for the power to live this seemingly impossible loving life-style that He calls me to, I need Jesus. But for this, I have had Jesus, and I am daily delighting in the fact that He is all that it takes.

Eric J. Fellman, former Moody Monthly *director, is an editor with the Foundation for Christian Living, Pawling, New York.*

Holy
by Eric J. Fellman

The frightening thing about God's holiness is that He holds it up as a standard for us: "Be ye holy; for I am holy" (1 Peter 1:16, KJV). Perhaps that's why we can relate so well to Isaiah's reaction when he was confronted by God's holy presence: "Woe is me! For I am undone" (Isaiah 6:5, KJV). In this atomic age, we might say, "This is it—I'm going to be vaporized!"

How can God ever expect us to mirror His holiness? It's a lifelong pursuit of climbing ever higher, even if we do not reach the summit. But I know the climb is possible because of how He's touched my life through the lives of others.

One such encounter took place in college. Working two jobs and studying Scripture primarily as a textbook had sent me to the bottom spiritually. A judgmental spirit gripped me; I approached our annual week of special meetings with a tree-sized chip on my shoulder.

One speaker was Vance Havner, an itinerant preacher, white-haired and slight of build. It seemed like the winter drafts in the auditorium could have knocked him down. But he began strongly, gripping the pulpit with power.

Then suddenly his shoulders sagged. His voice dropped its authoritative proclamation and fell to a whisper.

"I can't preach today," he said. "For the past five months, I've been going through the valley of the shadow of death, and I'm going to share some words from my heart, but no sermon. You see, I don't have any easy answers; I only hope what I say can lift the faith of some weary fellow traveler."

Dr. Havner tenderly recounted how he had lost his wife of thirty-four years. He said he had never known many of life's sorrows, but then came one year when he received more than he thought he could bear. He was "shipwrecked on God, stranded on omnipotence."

I listened intently, searching for the source of power that brought him through.

Sarah had died early one Sunday morning. Dr. Havner was scheduled to preach at a church. His theme, chosen before Sara died, was "Now Thee Alone."

He delivered his message that morning and included a short verse by Elizabeth Prentiss:

> Once earthly joy I craved,
> Sought peace and rest.
> Now Thee alone I seek,
> Give what is best.

Dr. Havner said one woman had approached him afterward and tearfully said. "How sorry we all are that you have lost Sara."

"Lost?" he gently responded. "No, my dear, Sara is not lost to me, *for I know where she is.*"

The power of that one phrase swept through the auditorium with all the blaze of Moses' burning bush. With tears in our eyes, we were captured by a sense of being on holy ground, led there by one who had gone before.

I sat in my seat long after the other students had left. Thanking God for breaking through what was a growing coldness in my heart, I asked Him to give me a measure of that same desire to know His heart.

Years later, I had another taste of His holiness while in Hong Kong on my way to mainland China. A friend took me down a narrow alley to a second-floor flat to meet a man recently released from prison in China. I knew I would be pressed to carry Bibles and literature on my trip. But I was hesitant and tried to mask my fear with rationalizations about legalities and other concerns.

A Chinese man in his sixties opened the door. His smile was radiant, but his back was bent almost double. He led us to a sparsely furnished room.

A Chinese woman of about the same age came in to serve tea. As she lingered, I couldn't help but notice how they touched and lovingly looked at each other. My staring didn't go unnoticed, for soon they were both giggling.

"What is it?" I asked my friend.

"Oh, nothing," he said with a smile. "They just wanted you to know it was OK—they're newlyweds."

I learned they had been engaged in 1949, when he was a student at Nanking Seminary. On the day of their wedding rehearsal, Chinese Communists seized the seminary. They took the students to prison.

For the next thirty years, the bride-to-be was allowed only one visit per year. Each time, following their brief minutes together, the man would be called to the warden's office.

"You may go home with your bride," he said, "if you will renounce Christianity."

Year after year, this man replied with just one word: "No."

I was stunned. *How had he been able to stand the strain for so long, being denied his family, his marriage, and even his health?* When I asked, he seemed astonished at my question. He replied, "With all that Jesus has done for me, how could I betray Him?"

The power of that holy life left its mark. The next day, I requested that my suitcase be crammed with Bibles and training literature for Chinese Christians. I determined not to lie about the materials, yet lost not one minute of sleep worrying about the consequences. And as God had planned, my suitcases were never inspected.

God uses the golden witness of His choicest saints to show us the journey toward holiness *is* possible, for others have gone before.

Chet W. Cady is a free-lance writer in Nashville, Tennessee.

Omniscient

by Chet W. Cady

When we brought Ben, our baby, home from the hospital, he turned out to be quite a theologian. He taught me about God's omniscience, though I thought I didn't have much to learn.

I'd been to seminary. I knew that omniscience is "the attribute of God whereby He knows all things." But that's only part of the definition, and stopping there made it easy for me to miss the implications. Scholars, however, have thought them through. So the definition goes on to say God knows all things "both actual and possible; past, present, and future; completely, perfectly, simultaneously, and eternally."

I could cite the Bible to prove God's omniscience. "And there is no creature hidden from His sight, but all things are open and laid bare to the eyes of Him with whom we have to do" (Hebrews 4:13). "The eyes of the Lord are in every place" (Proverbs 15:3). "His understanding is infinite" (Psalm 147:5).

I believed God was omniscient. Ben showed me how imperfect my belief was.

For months before he was born, I was upset about the way my life was turning out. I had graduated from seminary in the spring but still didn't have a pastorate by autumn. I was irritated about it—grumbling and complaining though I knew Scripture taught against my bad attitude.

Particularly difficult was seeing opportunistic and theologically unsound people with ministries. Friends from college went to liberal seminaries to learn disbelief in the Bible. They got churches. Students from my own seminary showed disregard for authority. They got churches. And every Sunday, television evangelists catered to what people wanted to hear—a gospel of health and wealth, with possibilities instead of sanctification—from their giant church-theaters.

The whole ministry-finding system seemed rigged against me. The classified ads in Christian magazines indicated churches wanted age (I was only twenty-nine) and experience (so much for that) in their pastors.

Churches judged pastoral candidates largely on their preaching. But it takes *practice* to be a good preacher. And with each month of not practicing what I preached (mirrors are not the same as congregations), I saw my shot at the pastorate slipping away.

I wondered how the stigma of my not being placed in a church right after seminary affects pulpit committees: "What's wrong with this guy? There must be some reason no other church wants him."

At summer's end, the equity from our house was gone. So when a Nashville publisher called and asked if I'd work temporarily on a project, I left Anna (pregnant with Ben and unable to travel) with her folks in Johnstown, Pennsylvania, and drove south in a car packed with essentials.

Then, one lonely night in Nashville, I got lost. It was the last straw. I blew up at God.

"All right, so I don't get a church. But why tear me away from Anna now and put me in a city where I don't know anyone? I've tried to obey Your Word and do what I understand it to say, and what do You do? You get me lost in a city I don't even want to be in! If You knew what this was doing to me, You wouldn't put me through it!"

I screamed that and more at Him, raging as I drove, lost in the dark.

Months later, I flew to Johnstown for Ben's birth, then returned. Three weeks after that, Anna and Ben joined me, and he started to show me how little I knew about God's omniscience.

Sometimes when we left him in his crib, he'd break out crying, apparently afraid of something. "Oh, Ben," I'd say. "If you only knew what your mother and I know about the situation, you wouldn't worry so. It's not as bad as you think."

23

He panicked when he got hungry. "Ben, you're not going to die," we'd reassure him in sympathetic tones. "If only you knew what we knew—that you won't die if you aren't fed at your first stirring of hunger."

Later on, after he'd matured some, we saw ire in his complaints. When we didn't let him do what he'd set his mind to—like biting electrical cords—he got mad.

I pitied Ben. His limited understanding evoked fear and outrage toward not only his circumstances but also his parents, even though we were looking out for him.

That was how Ben taught me about God's omniscience. I saw in Ben's immature mistrust of my knowledge a reflection of my own skepticism toward God's omniscience. I looked in his eyes and considered the impotence of his complaints in light of what I knew. How much punier, even contemptible, was my mistrust of God's *unlimited* knowledge.

Words I said to Ben about how he ought to trust my superior knowledge came back to mock me, as if God were saying, "Chet, if you knew what's really going on, you wouldn't worry so much. If you knew what I know, about how well things are going and how they'll turn out, you'd find it a hundred times easier to trust Me. If you knew now what you'll learn from this experience, you'd ask Me to put you through it. When it's over, you'll thank Me for it.

"Your comprehension will forever be limited, Chet. But time will show you how deep *My* understanding has always run. All I'm asking for is faith in advance of your fuller experience: trust Me now that I know what is best."

There's no room for oversight in God's knowledge. He doesn't forget. He doesn't blunder. He doesn't have to turn His attention from one fact to consider another. And He always knows the exact course of events to pace us through to bring about His desired result in us.

How unkind for me to have accused God of not understanding what I was going through. Of course He knew. He knew better than I did.

I'm not yet over wanting a pastorate, and I'm not sure I should be. So I still have to learn what God already knows about my vocation. But now I trust that He knows what's best, and I can wait for Him to prove it. After all, if Ben can trust my limited knowledge, then surely I can trust God's omniscience. That's not a bad lesson to learn from so young a teacher.

Ronald B. Allen is a profes-
sor of Hebrew Scripture at
Western Conservative Baptist
Seminary, Portland, Oregon.

Sovereign

by Ronald B. Allen

I was seated beside a lovely pond on the grounds of the Indonesian embassy in Singapore on the Friday after Thanksgiving, 1978. It was a bright, sunny day—and I was sick to my stomach.

The day had become a nightmare of red tape. I was en route from Taipei, Taiwan, to Kalimantan Barat (the western section of Borneo), where I was to speak at the annual field conference of the Conservative Baptist Mission in Indonesia.

My plan was to fly from Singapore to Kuching in the Malaysian part of Borneo, and from there to fly to Pontianak in Indonesian Borneo. A pilot with Missionary Aviation Fellowship would take me to the mission base.

In Singapore I was to get the ticket for the flight from Kuching, along with securing an Indonesian visa. So early that morning I went to the airline office, only to find it had moved back to Jakarta. One couldn't buy a ticket on that airline anywhere in Singapore.

Because my confirmed flight from Singapore to Kuching was on Air Malaysia, I next went to its office. The agent tried to help but wasn't able to get me a ticket. The best she could do was write a standby ticket and tell me I might be able to get one in Kuching.

With that, I went to the embassy for my visa. A gracious woman looked at my papers, studied my passport, but then stopped because I didn't have a confirmed ticket on the last leg of my trip.

I explained I couldn't get one in Singapore.

She went to her supervisor. When she returned, she told me her supervisor had confirmed my story. "He will stamp your passport on Monday morning at eight o'clock."

"But I need to have the visa stamp today. My flight to Kuching must be made this weekend, for the only flight to Pontianak from Kuching is Monday morning at eight. I'll miss every connection."

She responded, "I'm sure he just failed to notice. I'll go talk to him again." She was gone several minutes.

She returned distressed. "My supervisor will not stamp your passport

25

until Monday morning. He is already deviating from the policy by agreeing to stamp it without a clear airline ticket. He has face to save. I'm sorry."

He had to save face. She was sorry. I was stunned.

I told her about our sick daughter in Taiwan and that many people were counting on me. I told her how much it had cost for the ticket. I nearly told her the messages I had prepared for the missionaries.

That dear woman went to her supervisor for the third time. When she came back, she had a tissue at her eyes. She told me her supervisor would not change his mind, and if she bothered him once more, she would lose her job. "I'm really sorry," she said.

I left the office and sat beside the pond. It became a swamp for my emotions. I felt betrayed and alone. Even as I sensed God had forsaken me, I prayed to Him for help. Who else could I turn to?

I had to decide something. If I couldn't get to where I was going from Singapore, I'd try from someplace else. Jakarta, the capital of Indonesia, seemed the only place that made sense.

I went to the Air Garuda office in the embassy complex and asked if they would reserve a seat for me to Jakarta on a Monday morning flight. But the new ticket cost more than I had. I put a deposit on it, then rushed to the Air Malaysia office for a refund on the ticket I wouldn't be using.

The woman said she'd mail it to my home in Oregon. After hearing my story, she arranged for a transfer of funds to Air Garuda. With a credit card loan for the balance, I paid for the ticket, then went back to the embassy.

When the woman saw me again, she blanched. I told her my new plan; could I still get the visa stamp Monday? She said she'd do anything if she didn't have to talk to her supervisor again.

I spent the weekend in Singapore, enjoying the country and its people. Monday morning the woman gave me my stamped passport, and I flew to Jakarta.

I arrived after five. The airline office was closed. And I still didn't know how I would get to Kalimantan Barat. Even more, I didn't know where to stay that night, and my funds were getting low. I knew no one. I prayed to God.

Then I remembered a conversation months earlier with a missionary in Manila. He said, "If you ever get to Jakarta, you may wish to stay at the Central Mission Business Office run by the Christian and Missionary Alliance."

I found the address in the English section of the phone book, gave it to a taxi driver, and found myself on a long cab ride. Finally the driver pulled up, and I saw the sign for the mission.

I went in and introduced myself. The missionary who greeted me was incredulous: "You can't be Ron Allen!"

He said he'd been in radio contact with the missionaries where I was to speak and had learned the plane from Kuching wasn't flying that week. If I'd gone there from Singapore, I couldn't have got to Indonesia.

"We tried to find you all over Asia," he said. "We telephoned or wired every place we thought you might be, with no success. We wanted you to change your plans and come here to Jakarta. We've made arrangements for your flight to Pontianak from here, and we have a pilot waiting for the flight into the interior. Everything is ready, but we thought we would never see you."

Then he said. "Tell me, how in the world did you ever wind up here?"

How indeed. An official wanted to save face. A clerk was sorry. I was sick. But my God was there.

I responded, "The God I thought had rejected me, it was He who brought me here!"

You are a shield around me, O Yahweh, my Glorious One, who lifts up my head (cf. Psalm 3:3).

John Moore teaches Bible
and theology at Multnomah
School of the Bible, Portland,
Oregon.

Immutable

by *John Moore*

The crashing, rolling waves of the Pacific matched my thoughts and mood. One by one the waves rose out of the sea toward the gray, darkening sky, bringing the wash and roar of the sea, then folded back down on the sand and foam. The ocean seemed to spin with the mix of tide and surf, all in a random motion, without any seeming meaning or purpose. That seemed to fit; it seemed to match the horror of March 31, 1985.

It was a wet and cool spring day in Portland, and I was in the barn. The phone rang, and news came of an automobile accident. Our family quickly drove to the hospital. The next four hours seemed a blur, but they would not fade like a bad dream. The wife of one of our elders, also one of my close friends and colleagues, had had a bad accident. Despite the diligence of the hospital staff and the fervent prayers of many, she died.

As I dug my toe into the sand, my mind shifted back twenty years. As a young collegian I, too, had been in an auto accident. Many things were similar: the collision of two cars, the frantic work of firemen and paramedics, the quick, professional care of medical staff—and the death of my only brother.

As I walked that beach, it seemed that life was somewhat like those waves. Life itself rose up, reached for the sky, and then came crashing down on the surf and foam of time and mortality. In a world of change, where life is too brief, who is God? How is He the anchor of life during these times?

The writer of Hebrews stated: "Because God wanted to make the unchanging nature of his purpose very clear to the heirs of what was promised, he confirmed it with an oath. God did this so that . . . we who have fled to take hold of the hope offered to us may be greatly encouraged. We have this hope as an anchor for the soul, firm and secure" (6:17-19, NIV).

Life and, more important, God Himself were no different four thousand years ago. Here was Abraham, seemingly cast adrift in the land of Canaan. God had brought him out of Ur. He had seen the favor and forgiveness of the Lord in his marriage fears when he had tried to pass off Sarah as his sister, in his military conquests when God gave him victory over his enemies, and in his faith when he believed God would fulfill His promise and give him an heir through Sarah. And God had done it! The miracle of Isaac's birth documented the faithfulness of God.

But now Abraham faced perhaps the greatest challenge of his life. He sat beside his dead wife, mourning her death and recognizing that, despite God's promises to give him the land of Canaan, he owned no land in Hebron to even bury Sarah's body (Genesis 23). Yet amid Abraham's swirling life-sea, God remained the same. His promises were, and would be, fulfilled exactly in the terms of the oath and promise.

In our lives it is easy to forget but worth remembering: few things are forever. Fads and fashions, notions and nations, passions and possessions, even life on this planet all come and go. But God remains constant. He is unchanging—His promises and purposes will not change.

Life is a lot like the shadows that pass with the rotation of the day. At first glance they seem stable and constant. But careful observation reveals that they move. James notes that contrast: "Every good and perfect gift is from above, coming down from the Father of the heavenly lights, who does not change like shifting shadows" (1:17, NIV).

The fact of God's immutability, then, becomes the anchor or constant in a life of change. If God were to change, there would be only three alternatives: one, He could go from worse to better; two, He could change from better to worse; or three, He could change within Himself—that is, from immaturity to maturity. Yet, none of these are true.

Moses wrote, "God is not a man, that he should lie, nor a son of man, that he should change his mind" (Numbers 23:19, NIV). Isaiah noted, "I make known the end from the beginning, from ancient times, what is still to come. I say: My purpose will stand, and I will do all that I please" (46:10, NIV). The seemingly meaningless and tragic loss of a family member, or young mother, still fits into the purpose and plan of an unchanging God.

But what about the times when God appears to have changed His mind? The Lord was grieved and regretted the creation of man (Genesis 6:6). He relented, or changed His mind, concerning judgment on Israel at Mount Sinai (Exodus 32:14). God changed His mind about the impending judgment on Nineveh after its repentance—despite Jonah's prediction (Jonah 3:10).

Part of the answer to this seeming contradiction comes in realizing that

God does not always give us the complete terms of His judgment or prediction, not even in Scripture. In each of these three examples, the contrasting heart of repentance and godliness brought the reprieve of God. In all of the cases, the change is less in God and more in man. For God to change His conditional treatment of a situation as the character or intercession of man changes is precisely what His immutability dictates.

As I looked beyond the crashing waves and surf and up to the moon above the sea, I noted that the reflection of moonlight came down across the water and up to the wet sand at my feet. As I walked along, the moonlight stayed at my feet. Despite the crash and wash of the waves, that light still glistened and sparkled its brilliance from the heavens to my exact position. The wave action only enhanced the moonlight.

To a good extent, that is also the message of God's immutability. Despite our expectations and plans and the life spans given by God, which seem. like bouncing waves, He remains constant. He is the unchanging anchor who provides hope and encouragement, the light that burns through changing shadows. And He is the Savior and Lord who meets us in compassion and grace, who carries us through the waves of life as surely as He was in charge of the automobile accidents that have touched my life. For thousands of years, God's immutability has stabilized the saints of God in a world of constant change.

Elisa Morgan has a national radio ministry, "Considerations," sponsored by Denver Conservative Baptist Seminary.

Omnipotent
by Elisa Morgan

He sat to my right, holding a chicken salad sandwich as he talked. I knew well the thoughts and feelings behind his words, and yet they shocked me.

"If God is omnipotent, why doesn't He do something?" Single and thirty-eight years old, Phil wanted to be married. Just a month earlier, he thought he'd finally found her. But doubts blew cold air on their romance, and they broke up. He was angry, tired, and fed up with depending on a God who never seemed to fulfill His end of the bargain.

29

I'd been where Phil was. For four-and-a-half years, my husband and I waited to adopt a baby. After three-and-a-half years, I resigned my position as dean of women at a Bible college and went home to wait for the call at any minute.

It took a year, twenty-odd baby showers for other expectant mothers, hours of frittered-away time, and bushels of frustration for that call to come.

Like one driving a car with a bad clutch, I charged and braked intermittently. At times I attacked God's wisdom; at other times I submitted passively. But through it all I fumed, "Where is my all-powerful God, for whom nothing is impossible?"

Why doesn't an all-powerful God do what we want Him to? Why doesn't the God who opened up the Red Sea, gave sight to blind men, and walked across the Sea of Galilee give a thirty-eight-year-old single man a wife and a childless woman a baby?

Several answers have come to mind. Rabbi Rubenstein, a leading Jewish theologian who lived through the Holocaust, concluded God was absent. Another rabbi, Harold S. Kushner, in his book *When Bad Things Happen to Good People* determined God must be helpless to stop our tragedies. Still others view God as cruel and wicked, Someone who plays with people like puzzle pieces.

None of those alternatives satisfies me. But as I've wrestled with my all-powerful God's inaction in my life, I can't escape thinking about something I read by A. H. Strong concerning God's power. He wrote, "God can do all that He wills, but He will not do all that He can."

Two implications of this have kept me going as I try to come to grips with God's omnipotence. First, God won't do all that He can because He chains His power to His purposes. God's power serves *His* purposes, not mine. He never uses His power except to fulfill His purposes.

I don't know all of what God purposes for my life. I have no idea what specific results He will bring from those long years I waited to adopt a baby.

What I do know is that God wants to make me more like Jesus Christ. If He were to grant my every whim and fulfill every request the minute I made it, I'd end up resembling a tantrum-throwing child more than a mature woman.

As I see it, God uses His power for His ends and His desires. He carves away at our lives, matching us up to the image He has in mind for us. We can't interfere with this process. We can't demand He lay His purposes aside for our own. Because He has all power, He decides what we get and when.

The fact that God's power serves His purposes and not ours leaves some of us a little uneasy. When we see how power corrupts men and women who have it, we grow suspicious of God's use of power.

But God's power is different from the power we see around us. He doesn't do all He can not only because His power is chained to His purposes but also because it is coupled with His love.

The historian Lord Acton wrote, "O, it is excellent to have a giant's strength. But it is tyrannous to use it like a giant."

God possesses power greater than any giant. But He does not use His power like a giant. Rather, it is in the form of a man—born in a cattle shed, walking the shores of Galilee, mocked and spit upon, killed on a cross—that God extends His power. It's always clothed with love.

Now that we've received our baby, I've had a chance to grasp something of the parental love God has for me. I have the power to do just about anything two-year-old Eva wants. I can give her a pair of scissors when she squawks for them. I can allow her to play atop the picnic table on our concrete patio when she climbs precariously. I can give her cracker after cracker until her entire diet consists of crackers.

But I don't. My love constrains my power. Because I love her and don't want her to hurt herself, I don't give her everything she wants.

I also don't give her everything she wants because I don't want her to grow up to be impossible to live with. She doesn't understand. She gets frustrated with me. And I in turn get frustrated that she won't trust my love enough to obey. But because I love her, I won't give in to her.

God is not a vending machine. We cannot approach Him with the exact change of ten minutes of prayer, a 10 percent tithe, and ten seconds of waiting and receive our desired goods. He does not use His power for our purposes but for His. He does not use His power to meet our desires but to serve His love. Whether you're a thirty-eight-year-old man who wants to be married, a childless woman who wants a baby, a broken widow who wants her husband back, a frustrated worker who wants a worthwhile job, or a confused teenager looking for love, God's power can't be manipulated.

The all-powerful God doesn't do what we want Him to do because He has chained His power to His purposes and coupled His power with His love. Someday, when we've become all that He wants us to be, we'll look back and understand that part of His power lies in what He doesn't do.

Moody Press, a ministry of the Moody Bible Institute, is designed for education, evangelization, and edification. If we may assist you in knowing more about Christ and the Christian life, please write us without obligation: Moody Press, c/o MLM, Chicago, Illinois 60610.